1 WEEK
CORELDRAW
by S.A.H Adam

**THE SIMPLIFIED BEGINNERS' GUIDE
TO BECOME A DESIGNER IN 10 HOURS.**

**PLUS 90,000
RESOURCES**

This book belongs to

Name:

_____

Address:

_____

School:

_____

Class:

_____

Date:

_____

1 WEEK CORELDRAW

The simplified beginners' guide to become a designer in 10 hours.

100% GUARANTEED!!!

Table of Contents

Preface

To understand business, its greatness and achievements in its true perspectives. The study of business is very important to Business owners and business aspirants, which is applicable to Education aswell.

This work aims at providing wide range of standards to the notable aspects of business. Because, anything that is determined to be sold requires one or more impressions (showing it to the buyers) which is the first thing that happens the most whenever there are sales. The notable aim i am talking about is the meaningful appearance and attractiveness of that goods or services that you want to sell or render respectively. I have shortly put together in this book; a simple method that i used in the last summer to teach my students of under 10 and 15 years old, a 'how to design anything' in one week. Luckily for me and you, that experience was good enough for us and it made me feel happy to bring it to those who also deserve to have this knowledge in its simplest form. So i made this for beginners and i named it "One week CorelDraw".

This book and its method used by the author are very excellent to the extent that an under 10 student who can't handle some basic spellings was encouraged and confident enough to learn it and made good results after third week of starting the lessons.

In less than 3 weeks, under 15 students also provide better exports (the term used to publish designs from CorelDraw) and were happy for being able to learn it and they're proud enough to show what they have designed to their parents and fellow students.

It is not the aim of the author to have exhaustively mentioned their personalities. This is only to prove to you that your designs (and your ward's designs) are guaranteed after following these contents and never worried any more about studying the skills lessoned in this book. Except for professionalisation, because I don't stop learning too and I don't discourage learning more, never!!

So, brevity and simplicity have been the use of the author in explaining lessons and writing of this book.

INTRODUCTION

Each day of the first week is represented by a chapter, so day one is called chapter 1 until day five which is also called as chapter 5. Happily, you have two more days to make up for any uncompleted lessons, it is certainly one week CorelDraw (training).

Daily lessons will be listed before explanations. This is to make it easier for you because you have to memorize each keys to easily use them at anytime, it is not appropriate to search for your book or keys at every time that you want to use it. Rather, having memorized it is confidential, courageous and more appropriate. So, simply memorize the keys and I have made it easier for you to do.

Function keys are abbreviated as F keys. E.g. function keys 1, 2 and 3 are shortened as f1, f2 and f3, up to f12.

By the way, here's how to hold a mouse (the mouse has two buttons that are separated vertically, sometimes with a roll-able). Place your index finger on the left side button for left clicks, and place your middle finger on the right side button for right clicks, then use the remaining fingers to hold the mouse firmly to be able to move it around as much as you need. Make sure it's your right-hand (don't hold mouse with your left hand).

Control keys are also abbreviated as Ctrl keys. E.g. Control A will be shown as Ctrl + A, it continued up to control Z.

In addition, go to the top-area of your CorelDraw interface (just above your working area), simply right-click and check-mark all bars, so you can easily find and use them. After you've selected all, click-and-drag on the three-line at the edge of any bars to drag and arrange it as you like, or double click and click on the x to close/cancel any unwanted bars. Keep only toolbar at the left-side of your working area and keep only colours at the right-side.

How to place objects or images inside another object?

...Okay, select your image, click on EFFECT (at the top left of your screen), scroll down to POWER CLIP, click on PLACE INSIDE CONTAINER, now scroll to your working area and select the object that will contain your image.

Set it as you like to see it within the container, once satisfied with the preview, select CLOSE-CONTAINER at the bottom-left of your working area, if you want to re-adjust, select the container again and right-click, click on EDIT-CONTENT and adjust it as you like, then CLOSE-CONTAINER at the bottom-left again.

You may like to increase the outline weight to be sharp or bolder, select the object and click F12, choose your outline weight or size, sharp or curve edges, your preferred outline colour, once satisfied, select DONE or OKAY.

All function keys will be explained first. Let's get into it.

How to handle key-combinations

(it is always written as Ctrl + A to Ctrl + Z).

This is simple and it means; click on the ctrl button and then click on the next letter without lifting your finger from the ctrl until you have pressed both keys together. Yes, you got it! Remember, don't long press the letter keys, it is just a tap on the letter keys after holding the Ctrl key and then look at the screen.

If you don't get it (don't ignore it), read it once again and retry.

DAY 1

FUNCTION KEYS (F KEYS)

Just like I said earlier, function keys are abbreviated as F keys. E.g. function keys 1, 2, 3 and 4 are shortened as f1, f2, f3 and f4 respectfully, it continued up to f12 on all keyboards.

So, you have to memorize each function keys below with their meanings, which will facilitate your learning and implementation. Let's explain and practice these keys, and they are:

F1 ----- help

F2 ----- Zoom tool

F3 ----- Zoom out

F4 ----- Entire Page

F5 ----- Free-hand tool

F6 ----- Rectangle tool

F7 ----- Ellipse tool

F8 ----- Text tool

F9 ----- Full screen

F10 ----- Shape tool

F11 ----- Fountain fill

F12 ----- Outline pen

Explanations

1. F1 - CorelDraw help

This is the shortcut to finding helps on CorelDraw (click f1 on your keyboard) to view the help page and close it once you're done.

2. F2 - Zoom tool

After you clicked the F2 key, your cursor changes to a zoom tool. Thus, click and drag-through the area you intend to zoom (so, don't release the button/cursor until you have dragged the cursor across the area that you intended to zoom before you drop the button). In addition, you can also use letter Z without combining it with the ctrl key, it works as zoom tool as well.

3. F3 - Zoom out

This is used to view more areas beyond the current area (that you've zoomed-in earlier), jus with a single click on f3, you don't have to click and drag.

4. F4 - Entire Page (I love this function)

This function helps you to view everything on your page with a single click. May be you can't remember where you kept a text or image, and immediately you click on this function key (F4) you will be able to find whatever you have from anywhere on the screen.

5. F5 - Free-hand tool

This key freely allows you to draw a straight or curves lines anyhow you wish to draw it. After choosing this tool, two separate clicks (one after the other) will give you a straight line, click on ENTER button once satisfied. But, a single click-and-drag will give you a free hand drawing as you like.

6. F6 - Rectangle tool

This key allows you to draw squares, rectangles and their likes.

You may click and drag for your preferred shapes, you may have a single click on your working area to drop any shapes, and you can double click on its icon from the toolbox for a perfect page adaptive shape at the beginning of a new design, it will automatically adapt a shape to the portrait or landscape format on your screen.

To change the sharp edges to curve, click F10 you'll see small boxes at each edges for you to convert sharp edges to curve edges.

If it doesn't change, click ctrl+Q to convert line to curve, you must see the boxes 'now' convert your edges to curve (if you want to).

You can also merge shapes, one having sharp edges at a side and the other shape having curve edges, move one above the other, clearly seeing the 2 sharp edges and curved edges, click on Pick tool, the first tool on your tool bar (or click space-bar to drop the tool), now align both shapes and click on merge tool above your working space to merge both shapes/objects into one, good! You can also try it with a circle too.

In addition, you can also use ctrl+Q to convert a straight-line into a curve-line too, just select a line, click ctrl+Q and click F10 (shape-tool) to curve it or shape it as you like, use the arrow edges as well.

7. F7 - Ellipse tool
Ellipse tool also allows you to draw circle and its likes. You can also click and drag among others.

8. F8 - Text tool
After choosing the tool, with a click you are ready to type, just click anywhere on the screen. Similarly, if you click and drag you will be making a textbox.

9. F9 - Full screen
Easily preview your work on the full screen before you finally export your designs. Try it now.

10. F10 - Shape tool
This tool allows you to reshape any objects including: squares, images or texts.

11. F11 - Fountain fill
This key takes you to where you can fill your shapes or texts with; one color, two colors or multiple colors of your choice.

12. F12 - Fountain fill
This last function key allows you to increase the outer part of your object. Such as your texts, shapes or images, you can also change the outline color or width of your objects.

DAY 2

CONTROL KEYS (Ctrl A to G)

Ctrl + A ---- select all

Ctrl + B ---- brightness

Ctrl + C ---- copy

Ctrl + D---- duplicate

Ctrl + E ---- export

Ctrl + F ---- find

Ctrl + G ---- group

Explanation

Ctrl + A ----- select all

To pick all objects on your screen at a goal

Ctrl + B ----- brightness

To increase or decrease brightness of an object

Ctrl + C ----- copy

It is used to copy, so that you can paste that particular file or object to another place or another folder

Ctrl + D ----- duplicate

To have another immediate copy of the selected object(s) without losing the initials or originals

Ctrl + E ----- export

This is the action keys to share out your designs as an image (remember to choose .jpg, also jpeg format)

Ctrl + F ----- find

This command is used to find an object in an active document

Ctrl + G ----- group

To group and move two or more objects together at a time. (If you don't want to merge it into one).

DAY 3
CONTROL KEYS (Ctrl H to N)

Ctrl + H ---- Home

Ctrl + I ---- import

Ctrl + J ---- options

Ctrl + K ---- break apart

Ctrl + L ---- combine objects

Ctrl + M ---- use bullets

Ctrl + N ---- new page

Explanations

Ctrl + H ---- Home
This is to go to Front of Page

Ctrl + I ---- import
To bring or take objects into CorelDraw (like photo and background images, gifs or icons among others)

Ctrl + J ---- options
To opens the dialog for setting options

Ctrl + K ---- break apart
To breaks the selected object or text apart (separately), you can make a letter bigger than others or face any angle, you can as well use KNIFE-TOOL on objects (select it from the TOOLBAR)

Ctrl + L ---- combine objects
To combines the selected objects or text together again (after aligning you preferred text)

Ctrl + M ---- use bullets
You may also show/hide the bullet method of listing (it means using the dots [•] instead of numbers.

Ctrl + N ---- new page
To open a new page for creating another designs.

DAY 4
CONTROL KEYS (CTRL O to U)

Ctrl + O ---- open

Ctrl + P ---- print

Ctrl + Q ---- convert to curve

Ctrl + R ---- repeat

Ctrl + S ---- save

Ctrl + T ---- character formatting

Ctrl + U ---- ungroup

Explanations

Ctrl + O ---- open
To open another or previous accounts for designs

Ctrl + P ---- print
To print-out your designs (preview before you print!)

Ctrl + Q ---- convert to curve
To convert the selected object or lines from straight to a curve

Ctrl + R ---- repeat
To repeat the last operation or command (instead of creating all multiple designs from start, once you create one 'control + r' will help you repeat the design-with-the-last-action you performed).

Ctrl + S ---- save
To save the current design not to be lost

Ctrl + T ---- character formatting
For example; you want to do things like ¥ (Yuan) # (Naira) or $ (Dollar) on CorelDraw, use the single or double stroke among others.

So, after aligning the text, click both buttons.

Ctrl + U ---- ungroup
To ungroup the selected objects (and ungroup a grouped object).

DAY 5
CONTROL KEYS (Ctrl V to Z)

Ctrl + V ---- paste

Ctrl + W ---- refresh window

Ctrl + X ---- cut

Ctrl + Y ---- snap to grid

Ctrl + Z ---- undo

Explanations

Ctrl + V ---- paste

To paste the copied object or file into the selected area or design

Ctrl + W ---- refresh window

It is used to refresh the design or drawing window

Ctrl + X ---- cut

It is used to copy object to another area without keeping the originals or initials. Unlike Ctrl+C

Ctrl + Y ---- snap to grid

To snap objects to grid (or toggle between different options)

Ctrl + Z ---- undo

To reverse the last action or operation.

Also, use this link to get the video tutorials for each function keys on my YouTube channel. (They will be available eventually).

YouTube: BRIGHT NOTION

If need be, get in touch, or WhatsApp here 2348104168806.

Or send a request mail to rajidam100@gmail.com

inclusive of getting all the resources folder links forwarded to you.

COLOUR
CODES, COMBINATIONS
AND MEANINGS

What are plain background colours' meanings?

And what are the Best Color Combinations?

Due to copyright (©), the information had to be removed. So, download or bookmark the searched page linked here for you: https://www.tailorbrands.com/blog/logo-color-combinations

You'll have access to more than the information, including the illustrations, codes, meanings and practical examples among others.

Get designs samples here https://drive.google.com/drive/folders/1DB8_RnNdR3SPRiit5L2dg2xdYTZfw6_p
as you proceed to practice and taking assessments, you can choose any of these samples across all kinds of designs and practice.

Neither restrictions nor attribution of any kind required.

Download zip resources here https://drive.google.com/drive/folders/1c1sclfsU1ayALLRypgy5lORrJb1vRyB7
they will help to facilitate your designs.

Thus, more than 90,000 resources will be forwarded to you via the mail you made available to rajidam100@gmail.com.

You can also get this training workbook on Amazon!

DESIGN-DIMENSIONS GUIDES

CorelDraw supports all the dimensions you might need, such as; pixels, inches, centimetres, etc. However, some premium applications and resources provided for you only recognize dimensions in pixels or inches, etc.

Similarly, you might be ask or provided information in one format, while there's need to understand the exact dimensions in your software supported format.

You should learn how to get your precise resolution or visit unitconverts.net among others.

This is to avoid violation of copyright!

Afterwards, proceed to taking design challenges and practice with your teacher or trainer. If you're learning this yourself, look around you and take that designs for practice. Then, proceed to samples linked here for you and the workbook on Amazon.

20 COPYWRITING FORMULAS

The term "copy" has different meanings.
We would specifically discuss the first item on the list, which is copywriting.
However, before we go into the 20 copywriting formulae, let us first provide a brief overview of various types of copy.

1. Copywriting: Copywriting is the process of creating persuasive and compelling written material for advertising and marketing reasons. It also includes using language to promote a product, service, or concept and encourage the audience to take a certain action, such as making a purchase or subscribing to a newsletter.

2. Copy and Paste: Copy and paste is a common computer operation that allows users to copy text, pictures, or other stuff from one area (the source) and paste it into another one (the destination).

3. Copyright: Copyright is a legal term that gives the author of an original work the exclusive right to use and distribute it. This covers intellectual property such as literature, art, music, and so forth.

4. Copy in Journalism: "Copy" is the written text or story that a reporter or journalist creates for publishing in newspapers, periodicals, or internet media.

5. Copy in Design: In design, "copy" sometimes refers to the written text inside a layout or design, such as that seen in advertising, brochures, websites, and other graphic products.

6. Copying in Academics and Plagiarism: Copying in academics refers to the illegal use of another person's work, ideas, or words without due credit, which is termed plagiarism and is often unethical and intellectually dishonest.

As a result, to produce captivating communications for your target audience, you need to be familiar with more than just one or two formulae. Here are 20 formulae with examples of various items that can assist you in writing your text simply and fast outlining your products following the designs, or even utilising it with ease when making audio or video material targeted at advertising your brand, products and services.

Here are the 20 copywriting formulas and a few examples:

1. PAS (Problem, Agitate, Solve) - According to this formula, first identify the customer's problem, then emphasize the negative implications of not finding a solution, and then offer the remedy.

For instance, suppose you're utilizing this technique to sell Android phones.

Are you weary of sluggish, out-of-date cell phones that leave you irritated and separated from the outside world? It's time to say goodbye to those issues and embrace a cutting-edge solution that will revolutionize your mobile journey.

Problem: Consider the pain of attempting to access a webpage or use an app only to be met with continuous loading windows and slow performance. Your existing phone prevents you from keeping connected, losing valuable time, and becoming unproductive.

Agitate: Consider the missing chances and frustrations you had when you couldn't take that ideal shot or immediately receive and answer vital emails. The continual fight to keep up with the demands of contemporary living is taking a toll on your productivity, peace of mind, and affordability, as prices rise shortly.

Answer: Introducing our all-new Android phone, the ultimate answer to all your smartphone problems. This phone will change the way you engage with technology, thanks to its lightning-fast speed, smooth multitasking, and intuitive user interface. With the high-resolution camera, you can capture gorgeous photographs in real time, immortalising your cherished moments in clarity and detail. Every image, from spectacular scenery to bright selfies, will be a masterpiece.

Don't let your old phone limit your possibilities. Upgrade to our cutting-edge Android phone and open up a world of possibilities. Accept speed, efficiency, and seamless connectivity like never before.
Please click here to place your purchase right now.

2. FAB (Features, Advantages, Benefits) - To apply this strategy effectively, first define the consumer's problem, then promise to solve it with your product, then back up your claims with proof, and last encourage the buyer to act.

For instance, suppose you're utilizing this technique to market a suit.

Are you weary of wearing ill-fitting, boring clothes that don't leave an impression? Say goodbye to mediocre style and welcome a suit that oozes confidence and elegance, turning attention wherever you go.

Issue: Finding the ideal suit that combines immaculate elegance, superb craftsmanship, and a perfect fit may be difficult. Your present wardrobe lacks the refinement and effect you seek, making you feel underdressed and neglected in critical moments.

Promise: Introducing our premium suit, expertly created to boost your style and make a statement. We understand your need to be immaculately clothed, and our suit is tailored to your unique requirements.

Chracteristics: Our suit has a number of unique characteristics that set it different from the competition. Every element, from the highest quality materials to precision tailoring, is meticulously studied to achieve a great fit and outstanding comfort.

Advantages: Enjoy the benefits of wearing a suit that not only looks amazing but also feels fantastic. The airy fabric promotes flexibility of movement, while the attention to detail in the construction ensures durability and long-lasting quality.

Benefits: When you wear our outfit, you'll enter a world of advantages. Feel the boost of confidence as heads turn in awe of your flawless style. Command attention and create a professional and successful image in every setting.

Act today to update your wardrobe and improve your own style. Never settle for anything less than a suit that symbolizes your distinct personality and goals. Our premium suit is your ticket to refined elegance and timeless grace.
Order now.

3. PPPP (Picture, Promise, Prove, Push) - To apply this strategy effectively, first visualize the consumer's problem, then promise to solve it with your product, back up your promises with proof, and last urge the buyer to take action.

For example, suppose you're utilizing this method to sell clothing.

Picture: Consider the frustration of standing in front of your bulging closet, feeling as if you have nothing to wear. Your clothing don't represent your own style, and you have trouble finding ensembles that make you appear and feel confident.

Promise: Our excellent clothing selection will open up a whole new world of stylish choices. We vow to meet your style demands and supply you with clothing that will add to your wardrobe and raise your fashion game.

Prove: Our clothing is precisely crafted with attention to detail, utilizing high-quality fabrics that provide both comfort and longevity. Every stitch is expertly crafted, resulting in a flawless fit that flatters your shape and highlights your greatest features.

Push: Why settle for average when you can have extraordinary? Step into the world of fashion to showcase your individual style and create a big statement. Our garments are the key to opening up a world of limitless options and confidence-boosting looks.

Now is the time to take action and refresh your look. Upgrade your wardrobe with our unique range of stylish options. Embrace the confidence and empowerment that comes from wearing clothing that make you look and feel good.

4. USP (Unique Selling Proposition) - This formula focuses on identifying the distinguishing features of your product or service that set it apart from rivals and emphasizing them as the key selling point.

5. IDCA (Interest, want, Conviction, Action) - Similar to AIDA, this formula starts with capturing readers' attention and want, then focuses on gaining conviction and trust, and then moves on to the call-to-action.

6. 4-Ps (Product, Price, Promotion, and Place) - This formula is a traditional marketing framework that focuses on the four major components of a marketing strategy: simply define the product as a solution, followed by the price, promotion, and place (of distribution/access).

7. ACCA (Awareness, Comprehension, Conviction, Action) - This formula is frequently used in advertising campaigns that aim to educate the target audience about a product or issue, beginning with creating awareness, then to understanding the benefits, conviction (such as proofs and testimonials), and finally telling them to take action.

8. SOSTAC (Situation, Objectives, Strategy, Tactics, Actions, Control) - This is a comprehensive marketing planning framework that outlines the key components of a marketing plan, from assessing the current situation to defining objectives, creating a strategy, determining tactics, taking action, then monitoring and controlling the plan.

9. PASTOR (Problem, Amplify, Story, Testimony, Offer, Response) - This formula is frequently used in the context of direct response marketing and sales copy, with the goal of identifying the customer's problem, amplifying the problem pain, telling a story that resonates with the customer, sharing testimonials, presenting an offer, and encouraging a response.

10. 7-Ps (Product, Price, Place, Promotion, People, Process, Physical Evidence) - This is a variation of the 4-Ps framework that includes additional elements to consider in a marketing strategy, such as people (staff and customer service), process (how the product/service is delivered), and physical evidence.

11. SIVA (Solution, Information, Value, Access) - This formula is commonly used in B2B marketing, with the goal of presenting the product/service as a solution to the customer's problem, providing information that supports the solution, demonstrating the value of the solution, and ensuring easy access to (purchase) the solution.

12. CARP (Contrast, Action, Repetition, Pattern) - This formula is commonly used in the design of visual elements of advertisements or marketing materials, with the goal of using contrast to draw attention and encourage action, repetition to reinforce the message, and creating a visually appealing pattern.

13. SORC (Situation, Objective, reaction, Control) - This is a simplified version of the SOSTAC framework that focuses on the important components of a marketing strategy, beginning with analyzing the situation, identifying goals, selecting the intended reaction, and implementing control measures.

14. 5-Ws and 1-H (Who, What, When, Where, Why, How) This is frequently used in journalism and can be applied to marketing messages, focusing on answering the key questions of who the message is targeting, what the message is about, when and where the message will be delivered, why the message is important, and how the message will be communicated.

15. FEEL (Framing, Emotion, Evidence, Lead) - This formula is commonly used in copywriting and content marketing, with a focus on framing your message in a way that connects with your audience's interests, eliciting emotion, showing evidence to back your claim, and guiding audience to a desired action.

16. IDAC (Interest, desire, Action, Conviction) - Similar to AIDA and IDCA, this formula stresses generating interest and want, followed by a clear call-to-action, and finally gaining conviction and trust with the audience.

17. PPPP (Promise, Picture, Proof, Push) - This copywriting technique focuses on presenting a clear promise to the audience, utilizing vivid imagery to build a picture, offering proof to back the promise, and encouraging audience to take action.

18. FAB (features, Advantages, Benefits) - This is commonly used in sales and marketing to emphasize a product or service's essential qualities, describe the benefits featured, and finally demonstrate how those benefits benefit the consumer.

19. PPP (Promise, Picture, Proof) - Like the PPPP formula, this one emphasizes presenting a clear promise to the audience, employing vivid imagery to paint a mental picture, and offering proof to back up the promise.

20. RACE (Reach, Act, Convert, Engage) - This formula is frequently used in digital marketing and emphasizes the key stages of a digital marketing funnel, beginning with reaching the target audience, encouraging them to act (for example, by visiting a website or filling out a form), converting them into customers, and then engaging with them to maintain the relationship.

It's vital to note that these formulae aren't a one-size-fits-all approach to developing great marketing messaging. It is critical to understand your target demographic, goals, and brand personality, as well as to experiment and iterate on your marketing strategies to determine what works best for your unique circumstance.

As always, it's important to remember that these formulas are simply guidelines. The most effective marketing and advertising messages are tailored to the specific audience and situation, and are constantly being refined and optimized through experimentation and iteration.

18 SALES OBJECTIONS; HOW TO ANALYSE THEM, AND TIPS TO HANDLE EACH OBJECTIONS:

1. Unspoken Objection:

- How to identify:

The first type of objection you will get can most likely be an unspoken objection, this is when the customer has concerns with your offer but doesn't message you or tell you anything.

- Handling: The solution is to let the prospect talk more. Ask him/her open-ended questions, and listen intently to the answers The more prospects answer your questions, the more exactly you'll identify what might be holding them back from buying. Thus, using your offer as the solution to their pain-points and close the sale.

  You can ask questions like:

    Misses___,

I can help, so what do you want to accomplish? What do you try to fix this situation?

How do you live this dissatisfaction daily?

Did it work or not?

And why not get this proven solution?

What would your life be like if you get what you're searching for?

What else are you looking for?

Why are you unsatisfied?

Use questions like these to dig deeper regarding the problems announced by your potential clients because your main goal is to understand the emotions associated with their specific problems and solve it for them at your profitable price!

"I'll get back to you":

This response is a very popular objection that make many people lose their sales, but not you anymore. I could put it as numbers one on this objections handling list because it's mostly used than other objections (of course it's number one objection in response) but I added it between, and after the unspoken objection because I know it and I can guide people about it. Most times this objection "I'll get back to you" isn't sincere/real! Don't let your prospects/clients go away, understand why it's not now and why or when he's getting back to you with the followjection tips below.

You can ask questions like:

What would it take for you and I to do business today?
(This let him share his why so you can get the real objections and know when next or what next to do)!

Is it the term?

Is it the money?

Is it the price? Or,

It is the time?

What part of the deal you don't like?

Once again, the key is to identify the real objection, fix it and close the sale my dear!

2. Price/Cost Objection:

- How to identify:

Is when your prospect expresses concerns about the affordability or high cost of your product/service.

- Handling: First highlight the values/benefits of your products, create offer options associated with his wants or needs, like adding more relevant bonuses to increase the perseved values and never reduce your price unnecessarily, except for specific concerns about
the price.

What happens when you retain prices for your good values and

profits?

You gain clients' emotional investments!
Your clients value your service more!
You filter and attract best clients, they're easiest to satisfy and cost less to fulfill, they preferred to choose you again for relative values!
You multiply your revenue margin because you have money to invest and create efficiency; improved customers experience; and scale your business! Etc.

But, when you decrease your prices:

• You decrease your clients' emotional investment since it didn't cost them much.
• You decrease your clients' perceived value of your service since it can't be that good if it's so cheap, or priced the same as everyone else.
• You attract the worst clients who are never satisfied until you have decreased more or your service is free.
• You've destroyed the margins you'll get to be able to provide an exceptional services, afford best tools, invest in growth, or scale more!

3. Timing Objection:

- How to identify: When a prospect indicates that the timing is not right for making a purchase at the moment, or that your offer duration is too short.

    - Handling: Identify priorities, demonstrate long-term value and use their valid excuse to extend your offer duration, thus emphasize the consequences of further delay in their buying decision.

4. Product Fit Objection:

    - How to identify: The prospect questions whether your product/service is suitable for their specific needs.

    - Handling: Ask probing questions to understand their concerns, provide tailored solutions, and share relevant success stories or testimonials of people that have used the products.

5. Competition Objection:

    - How to identify: your prospect brings up concerns about your competitors' creating offers on same product.

    - Handling: Focus on your unique, offer a trust and guarantee by helping them to achieve their goals, and address his specific concern about the competition and you'll get the contracts or sales.

6. Trust Objection:

- How to identify: The prospect expresses doubts or lack of trust in your product/service.

    - Handling: Establish your credibility and believe in the product, present success stories and testimonials, offer him guarantees, and address trust concerns openly.

7. Need/Relevance Objection:

- How to identify:
When prospect questions the necessity or relevance of your product/service to their specific situation.

    - Handling: Ask open-ended questions to understand their needs better, highlight the unique benefits and solutions your offering provides, and provide relevant examples or case studies.

8. Risk Objection:

  - How to identify: Your prospect expresses concerns about potential risks or negative consequences associated or experienced with your previous product/service.

    - Handling: Appreciate their expression on previous experience, inform him about unawares, address their specific concerns about risk by offering guarantees, present testimonials from satisfied customers, and provide reassurance that emphasize how you mitigate potential risks.

9. Lack of Urgency Objection:

- How to identify:

When your prospect doesn't see a compelling reason to make a buying decision quickly.

    - Handling: Create a sense of urgency by 1- highlighting limited-time offers (can be: waiting list, prelaunch or earlybirds offer), 2- upcoming price increasement, 3- the potential benefits they might miss out on by delaying the buying decision. Thus, paint a clear picture of the positive outcomes they can achieve by acting promptly.

10. Budget Objection:

    - How to identify: Your prospect states that they don't have the budget or financial resources to proceed.

    - Handling: Create flexible payment options, making it affordable and easier to purchase, hook him on long-term value by paying twice or thrice without losing your offer and bonuses if the payment start now.

11. Skepticism Objection:

- How to identify:

A prospect shows skepticism or doubt about your claim or promise.

    - Handling: Provide facts, customer testimonials, or third-party endorsements to support your claims. Offer a free trial if possible or offer a product/services that'll make him want more, believing he'll come back to you, and showcase the effectiveness of your product/service.

12. Change/Disappointment Objection:

- How to identify: Your prospects resist on making a change from their existing plug/solution-provider.

- Handling: Understand their current challenges and pain points, then highlight the limitations of their current solution, Now present trust and guarantee, then offer a smooth plan and provide excellent customer support during the changeover.

Remember, objection handling is not about forcefully convincing prospects but rather understanding their concerns, providing relevant information, and finding solutions that address their specific needs. So, adapt your approach based on the objection and the prospect's individual situation to increase your chances of overcoming objections and closing more sale successfully.

Alright, let's continue...

13. No Authority/Decision-making Objection:

- How to identify: The prospect states that they lack the authority or decision-making power.

- Handling: Politely ask for introductions to relevant decision-makers, offer to provide information or materials that can be shared with them, and schedule follow-up meetings that may involve all key stakeholders.

14. Time Constraint Objection:

- How to identify: The prospect claims to have limited time available for engaging in the buying process and only need verified solution as quick as possible. (This is a common behaviour of people who buy luxurious products, so prepare for them).

- Handling: Highlight the efficiency of your product/service in saving their precious time, provide concise and targeted information, offer flexible meeting options (e.g., virtual calls, quick link or quick demos), and emphasize the potential time-saving benefits they can gain by using your solution.

15. Doubt in Vendor's Capability Objection:

- How to identify: The prospect expresses doubts about your company or a creator's capability to deliver as promised.
- Handling: Appreciate all prospects that give time to share their feedbacks, helps or experience, talk things that interest such customers if you have any, Share success stories, customer testimonials, or case studies that demonstrate your company's track record, expertise, and reliability. More so, offer guarantee and references to other satisfied customers who can defend and testify for your capabilities.

16. Product Complexity Objection:

- How to identify:
 A prospect finds your product/service too complex or difficult to understand.
- Handling: Simplify your messaging and explanations, provide clear and concise demonstrations, offer training or support resources like a summary bonus, and focus on the most relevant and impactful benefits and features that align with their specific needs.

17. Perceived Lack of Value Objection:

- How to identify: Your prospect questions the value or benefits they will gain from your product/service. (They may not be price-driven customers or luxurious-product buyers. But, they're the most common; they buy the values or benefits they'll gain from your products/services).
- Handling: Engage in a thorough needs analysis to understand their pain points, present personalized solutions that directly address their challenges, quantify the potential return on investment, and provide real-life examples or success stories that highlight the value others have achieved from the same product/services.

18. Perception of Implementation Challenges Objection:

- How to identify:
 Another prospect's concerned about the complexities or difficulties involved in implementing your solution before seeing results.

- Handling: Summarize/outline your implementation process, guide him on what's next and help to simplify the process, add some bonus resources provided, and share success stories of other customers who have successfully implemented your solution strategies. Also address their specific concerns and offer reassurances that you will be there to support them every step of the way.

HOW TO GET
LEADS OR CLIENTS ORGANICALLY

1. Write a good and interesting copy about your services, putting your interested clients and their interests first, send a minimum of 5 to 10 cold DMs everyday for one or two weeks. Resulting into 50 or 100 DMs per week, you'll get some clients quickly and others eventually.

2. When you see a work you can do for any personal or business brands perfectly, do it for free, send it to them, don't ask for a pay, ask them, and your happy clients to post and recommend you to their network or followers, you'll receive more clients coming to you with trust and they are interested, then keep them and sell them your services at your profitable price.

3. Use platforms like; LinkedIn and Twitter (now X) among others, their algorithms are friendly, create very appealing post or giveaway designs services and ask them to retweet or reposts. When anyone comments or reshares your posts his network or followers will be notified, so you'll get more impressions/views and resulting into more clients and more orders.

4. Also, search for "graphic design" on linkedin, click on jobs or services, scroll down and turn on notification for graphic design jobs. You'll be notified about new jobs from brands almost everyday.

5. Occasionally, when you have great designs for yourself or clients, or reviews among others, never deny yourself the ability to post about it to attract more clients and leads, don't focus on the negatives thoughts, but the positives and understand your community better.

6. Engage with other people's posts, you'll get more profile visits, then more impressions and leads. Also, engage and speak on spaces like Twitter space and co, there are powers in your voices than you may think.

7. Create valuable and informative content in any form: Blog posts, videos, infographics, or podcasts. And share your expertise, address common pain points of your target audience, also use SEO strategies to make your content discoverable for searches.

8. Build an email list of interested prospects and send them regular newsletters or updates. Provide value in your emails by sharing insights, tips, and special offers.

9. Host spaces, webinars, or workshops on topics related to your industry. These events can showcase your expertise and attract participants who are interested in your services.

10. Partner with complementary businesses to cross-promote each other services. This can expand your reach to a new audience too.

11. Implement a referral program where existing clients are rewarded for referring new clients to your business. Incentives can include discounts or other benefits that will interest them.

12. Write guest posts for reputable blogs in your industry. This will help you get a wider audience and establish authority.

BONUSES RESOURCES

Graphic design materials

Here is a list of websites for any resources
you may need as a designer

MOCKUPS

http://www.psdcovers.com/

http://www.psds.co http://www.fribbble.com

http://www.premiumpixels.com

http://www.teehanlax.com/tools/iphone

http://www.teehanlax.com/tools/ipad/

http://www.mockuuups.com

http://freebiesbug.com/

https://marvelapp.com/resources/

http://uispace.net

http://dbfreebies.co

http://365psd.com/ http://pixelbuddha.net/

http://pixelsdaily.com/

BAGROUND IMAGES

http://br.freepik.com/

http://www.shutterstock.com/

http://www.deviantart.com/

http://www.morguefile.com/

http://www.sxc.hu/

http://openphoto.net/

http://www.photorack.net/

http://www.unprofound.com/

http://www.freedigitalphotos.net/

http://www.freefoto.com/index.jsp

http://www.freepixels.com/

http://www.everystockphoto.com/

http://www.flickr.com/search/advanced

http://unsplash.com/

http://superfamous.com/

http://littlevisuals.co/

http://splitshire.com/

https://us.fotolia.com/

https://visualhunt.com/

https://www.pexels.com/

http://epicantus.tumblr.com/

https://stock.tookapic.com/

http://jaymantri.com/

http://snapwiresnaps.tumblr.com/

http://freestocks.org/

http://getrefe.tumblr.com/

http://nos.twnsnd.co/

https://picjumbo.com/

http://superfamous.com/

http://deathtothestockphoto.com/ http://www.lifeofpix.com/

http://search.creativecommons.org/ http://www.photl.com/

https://photodune.net/

http://littlevisuals.co/

http://www.splitshire.com/

http://negativespace.co/

http://www.stockvault.net/

http://www.gratisography.com/ https://stocksnap.io/

http://jeshoots.com/

http://br.123rf.com/

http://pixabay.com/

http://cupcake.nilssonlee.se/

http://www.uhdwallpapers.org/ http://kaboompics.com/

http://foodiesfeed.com/

http://www.raumrot.com/10/

http://jaymantri.com/

VECTORS | ICONS | PATTERNS

http://br.freepik.com/

http://www.fordesigner.com/

http://medialoot.com/

http://graphicburger.com/

http://psdblast.com/

http://subtlepatterns.com/ http://designm.ag/resources/650-free-photoshop-patterns/

FONTS

http://www.dafont.com/pt/

http://www.1001fonts.com/

http://www.google.com/fonts

http://www.netfontes.com.br/

http://www.fonts.com/

http://www.fontsquirrel.com/

http://www.myfonts.com/

http://www.myfonts.com/WhatTheFont/

http://okaytype.com/hello/friend

https://typekit.com/

Design Template Such As Flyers

http://www.freepik.com/

http://www.freepsdflyers.com/

https://free-psd-templates.com/

https://graphicsfamily.com/

https://psdfreebies.com/

https://downloadpsd.cc/

https://365psd.com/ https://all-free-download.com/

AI ENGINES

1. Docktopus Al: Create compelling slides for your presentations with Al.
2. Promptpal Al: Helps you discover the best Al prompts.
3. Quinvio Al: Create video presentations using Al.
4. Ask Your PDF: An Al Chatbot that helps you interact with PDF document.
5. Supernormal Al: An Al-powered meeting recorder.
6. Suggesty Al: Get human-like answers to your Google searches with GPT-3

7. ChatGPT Sidebar: ChatGPT Chrome extension that can be used on any website.

8. MarcBot: An AI assistant that lives inside Telegram.

9. Motion AI: Easily build chatbots to do anything on any platform.

10. Roam around: Plan your trips through AI travel planner.

11. Beautiful: Generative AI presentation app for the workplace.

12. Quotify: AI-powered tool to extract meaningful quotes from books and articles.

13. Harvey AI: An AI-powered legal advisor.

14. Beary AI: An AI tool to read, write and create content.

15. Scispace AI: Your AI research assistant to save hours per day.

16. Hints AI: GPT based AI assistant helps you to use productivity tools more efficiently.

17. Monday.com: Build your ideal workflow with 200+ customizable templates using AI.

18. Base64 AI: Extract text, data, photos and more from all type of docs using AI.

19. Al Article Writer: Generate articles and blog posts with Al in seconds.

20. Engage Al: Use Al to write insightful comments on Linkedin.

21. Google Duplex: An Al-assistant that can talk to you on your phone.

About The Author

RAJI, Adam Olanihun is an experienced graduate in graphic designs and most especially CorelDraw designs from God's Technology, Badagry, Lagos State, Nigeria. He is a graduate of the Better-by-far University, University of Ilorin, Ilorin, Kwara State, Nigeria. He hails from Mondu compound, Oke-Oyi, Ilorin, Kwara State, Nigeria.

He achieved the reputation "ADAM ROYAL HONESTY" after tens of years in his Arabic and Islamic studies boarding school, for always being honest at all costs.ays being honest at all costs.ays being honest at all costs.ays being honest at all costs.

He is a Muslim and he's married and currently blessed with a child, may the Almighty guides his parents, teachers, sibling, friends, wife, and bless him with pious childrens, and increase him in blessings.

Thanks, and anticipate more of his books.